TABLE OF CONTENTS

INTRODUCTION

Breeders often receive emails from people who are interested in breeding cats. More often than not, these people just want to have "one litter," because they want their children to experience the "miracle of life" and they have all sorts of friends who would want a kitten. So they believe they will not have any problems placing the kittens. Additionally, they often believe they will be able to easily obtain stud service for their female cat. Every breeder has a litany they go through when it comes to talking to these "I just want to have one litter or two" would-be breeders. Sometimes, it comes off a bit terse due to previous bad experiences, or breeders who are just tired of people who think they can make some money breeding cats. Some breeders just delete/ignore the would-be breeders out of exasperation.

It is a tough position for a reputable breeder to find themselves in. As a whole, many do want to encourage and help new breeders in the process in order to help continue and preserve the breed. Additionally, showing breeders are all too aware of the downturn in registration numbers and would like to reverse that trend and grow the number of people (and cats) in our hobby. However, any breeder that has been breeding for more than a few years has probably had at least one bad experience with a new breeder. Bad experiences include lack of communication (the new breeder just disappears after getting a cat), poor care of the cat (resulting in severe illness or death of the sold cat), or just generally disappointing (the new breeder doesn't show, or resells the cat, or perhaps even over-breeds the cat.)

This book is meant to be a guide for future, would-be breeders. It's also meant to help existing breeders when faced with an inquiry from a new breeder (it can be used as a response rather than having to take the time to write it out or talk it out for each inquiry.) It will be geared specifically toward the Persian breed, but will still be applicable to other breeds

Before You Start - Consider This

Before you even start searching for your first cat to breed, there are number of important details to consider. First, especially in light the shaky economy, is finances. In Persians, a nice show quality cat generally starts around $1500 and can go well over $3500 (depending on pedigree, titles, ect.) This is for a single cat. A basic program needs 1 male and 2-3 females. Most would-be breeders assume they will only need a single female and acquire stud service for her, but you will quickly find out that stud service is not the norm in the cat fancy. Those breeders that do allow stud service are generally not the homes you would want your female to be living in to be bred. Additionally, there is the cost of care, upkeep, and showing. Breeding cats should be feed premium foods, which generally cost between $1-$5 a pound. Breeding cats also do better when the dry "kibble" food is supplemented with a raw meat diet. A good quality meat can run from $1-$5 a pound (and this varies wildly in availability). There are also bowls, litter, litter pans, and medical supplies to consider. Vet visits are a must, whether is a check-up with a new cat, or the inevitable illness. Certain medicines should be kept on hand to quickly deal with the smaller problems that might come across. On average, the upkeep of a single Persian can run about $50 a month – that is assuming there are no major medical problems such as a c-section (an emergency C-section can cost $2000 easily). If the cat is being shown, an additional $200 per show week (minimum) must be factored in. (Most shows require travel, and many will require overnight stays in hotels. This all adds up!)

If you have already purchased your first cat(s) for breeding, pause a moment to consider the quality of your first cat(s). Did they come from breeders who are actively showing and getting titles (Grand Champion, minimally) on their cats? Have you shown your new cat(s) yourself? A pitfall many new breeders find themselves in is making their first purchase(s) impulsively. There are, unfortunately, many unscrupulous breeders who are easily found via web searches who will sell anyone with enough money a "breeding" cat - they might even call it a "show quality" cat, even if the breeder themselves is not actively showing. Sometimes these unscrupulous breeders will point out the many "Champions" on a pedigree and use that to indicate good breeding type. Please be aware the title of "Champion" in CFA is a title achieved without competition. It is simply awarded to a cat that attends one show and is not disqualified in at least 6 rings. The "Champion" title is not an indication of good quality in a breeding line and should generally be dismissed outright. More about titles will be discussed further on in this book. However, if your first cat(s) are clearly not near the written standard, it is advisable to neuter/spay and start over with quality cats. Otherwise, most top breeders are not going to consider you for placement of their cats, as they want their cats to be used in top quality breeding programs. If you aren't sure if your first cat(s) meets the standard, the best way to find out is to actually show your cats.

Next, you have to consider your home environment. The cats will need their own space. Plus, you will need to have an isolation area for any new cats that come into the home environment. Ideally, cats should be housed in a part of the house with their own ventilation, but should this not be possible, you will have to consider how you will keep them in their home in a healthy and safe environment. Whole male cats have a very strong odor to their urine that can quickly spread to the entire home (even if they are using the litterbox and not spraying,) so you will have to consider how will ventilate your home so that doesn't happen.

There is also the consideration of what laws regulate the area in which you live. Most cities have limits on the numbers of pets that can live in a household. While most breeders operate "under the radar," – and cities tend to leave them alone if they are not a nuisance - you should at least know what the laws are in the area in which you live.

Next, you will have to consider what you will do with the kittens you produce. Those friends you had before you bred the cat might have changes in their lives. They might decide that it's just not the right time to have a kitten. They might also have found a cat elsewhere while you were going about the business of getting a breeding cat and raising the litter. (Most breeders don't like keeping waiting lists because that is exactly what happens – the people who say they will wait rarely actually do wait.) It's possible you might have a "special" needs kitten that will not be an "easy" keeper; then you end up having to keep that kitten yourself.

Finally, there is the emotional toll that raising any animal to consider. Will you be able to accept the possibility of kittens dying? Is your heart strong enough to mourn the loss of a kitten that you held in your hands and watched it take its last gasp and then be able to face the next kitten, the next possible loss? Breeding animals is heartbreaking... losses are inevitable, and sometimes unavoidable. Sometimes the losses are avoidable, but caused by a mistake you make. New breeders are bound to make mistakes that will cost the lives of the kittens they brought into the world. This is a harsh, painful reality. Beyond the loss of kittens, there is also the parting with the kittens you have raised when it is time for them to go to new home. Of course, you will develop an emotional bond with a kitten have raised since birth and letting them go isn't as easy as it seemed it would be when you first thought of the idea of raising cats. Keeping too many kittens is a common mistake made by new breeders who quickly find themselves "over-catted" and overwhelmed by the work it takes to keep up all those cats. Even if you find yourself capable of coping the losses and letting kittens go, the third area that new breeders tend to encounter problems with is with the breeding cats themselves. They tend to keep them too long and then end up with a "top heavy" number of cats – where they have more cats that are not breeding than are, and again, this can lead to a situation where the breeder is overwhelmed by the number of cats they have to care for.

There are other concerns as well. If you have a significant other, it's very important they are "on board" with the idea of breeding and raising cats. If you are showing your cats, someone often has to stay behind to care for the cats left in the room (especially if you happen to have a new litter at the time.) Cleaning litter boxes, vacuuming, scrubbing, and bathing cats might not really appeal to your significant other, and this can lead to issues far more complicated that just the cats.

Also, if you have children, you have to consider the time the care of your cats will take from your children. Many families incorporate their children with the care of the cats, which can teach responsibility and respect for animals, as well as giving them a hobby that many children learn to love. In the show hall, older children can often be engaged as ring stewards (disinfecting judging cages between cats) and this can earn them extra money for whatever they might want to buy. However, if your children do not want anything to do with the cats, then they can be more of a source of friction than fun.

STARTING YOUR SEARCH

If you have considered all of the possible issues that you might encounter when breeding and you think you are really ready to be a cat breeder, then your search for a cat is the next step. Luckily, in the internet age, all you need to start is at your fingertips. CFA maintains a breeder referral list, but the best place to start is by visiting local shows and meeting breeders in person. Also, you can look at CFA's website and find the top cats winning cats.   Note the cattery names that produced the top winning cats of your breed, then search the web to find their websites and/or social media pages.

Ideally, you want to find the websites of breeders and look at their cats. Look at the pictures. If the website pictures any cats that are not clean and well-presented, move on. Most catteries put up pictures of their cats only when they think they look nice. So if a cat looks dirty and that was what the breeder thought looked nice, that is definitely not a good sign of a breeder you want to purchase a cat from. Of course, good looking cats in pictures is no guarantee, either, so remember to always listen to your gut and watch for red flags.

Next, look for titles on the cats used in and/or produced by their breeding program. Depending on the organization, the titles will vary, so be sure to make sure you know which organization the titles were achieved in. In CFA, a cat that achieves a "CH" (Champion) title is basically a cat that probably didn't defeat any other cats and simply was not disqualified in 6 rings. This isn't a title that means much about the real quality of the cat. The next title up is "GC" (Grand

17

Champion.) This requires defeating 200 other cats that are not yet Grand Champions themselves. This title is definitely a good indication of quality. Ideally, the cat's pedigrees should have more GC than CH or no title at all. There are also the titles of "PR" and "GP" (Premier and Grand Premier), which are the equivalent of CH and GC, but these titles are won by a cat that has been neutered or spayed. Other titles include "RW" and "NW" (Regional Winner and National Winner, respectively). These titles are much harder to achieve than GC and should be given considerable weight in a pedigree. There is also the title of "BW" (Breed Winner) which is only awarded to one cat in each breed (or Persian division) each season. Like RW and NW, this title carries significant weight. Finally, there is the title of "DM" (Distinguished Merit) which is found at the end of a cat's name. This title means the cat has produced either 15 (if it is a male) or a 5 (if it is a female) cats that have become GC or GP. This is often called the "breeder's title" because it is indicative of a cat that can produce quality cats. This is a title that breeders really look for as it is an indicator that a line can produce quality cats consistently.

It is worth repeating that seeing these titles does not mean every cat produced from those lines will be worthy of showing and/or breeding. You will want to find cats that have those titles within 1-2 generations – if those titles only appear 4 or more generations back, that probably isn't a breeder you want to purchase a cat from.

You also want to see if the breeder has produced cats that can at least achieve the GC title. This is a good indication the breeder is aware of the written standard for their breed and capable of producing cats that meet that standard. Even better, look to see if other breeders have been able to show cats produced by that breeder to at least the GC title. Look to see how cats from that breeder have produced for other breeders. Are their lines consistent? Do they make nice kittens when mixed with other lines? Can other people show them and still win? These are all important questions when it comes to researching the breeders of cats you like. Remember, nothing is a perfect indicator of a good breeder. Trust your instincts if you feel like you are being misled.

Ideally, you would want to find a breeder that lives relatively near you geographically. This allows you to either visit the breeders home (but don't expect a tour of their cattery) and get a feel for how they care for their cats, as well as to be able to see the cat in person before purchasing it. Picking up a cat at the airport often leaves you with few options if you are not happy with the quality of the cat, especially if the cat was purchased from a breeder in another country. Unfortunately, many breeders refuse to sell breeding cats to people who live in the same area as them. These breeders are not the kind of breeders you would want to purchase from, anyway, as their own greed and jealousy of wins in the show ring has overcome any desire they might have had to help new breeders. They do not sell in their area because they feel like they have to control what cats from "their" lines are in the shows possibly competing against them. It's a sad mentality and not healthy for the cat fancy as a whole, so I do not recommend supporting their policies by purchasing a cat from any breeder that has such ridiculous ideas about manipulating competition by placing restrictions on where they sell their cats.

Most breeders will place a copy of their sale contract and/or health guarantee on their website for potential buyers to read before inquiring. Read those contracts! It's very important to know what is spelled out in them before you even consider sending them an inquiry. Every breeder will have a different contract, though you will find there are some parts of the contracts that are similar from breeder to breeder. Many breeders restrict where the offspring of the cat can be sold – again, this isn't a policy that is healthy for the cat fancy, and I do not condone supporting those breeders by purchasing their cats. A standard contract should include some sort of health guarantee, outline expectations for the standard of care of the cat by the buyer, and what is to be done with the cat should the buyer no longer wish to keep the cat in their breeding program. If you do not agree with a breeder's contract, you can ask for them to consider making changes, but never, never buy a cat intending to break a contract. Although some contracts are completely ridiculous, if you choose to buy the cat and sign the contract, you should abide by what you agreed to. Breaking a contract is a quick way to establish yourself on a black list for all breeders.

Again, it is a good idea to attend at least one cat show, possibly more, in your area to meet local breeders and observe the process of showing. It's possible that many breeders there will be busy showing their cats and/or perhaps naturally a bit shy and unwilling to talk between judging rings, but you can learn a lot just by watching and listening. Don't be afraid to ask questions. You can even bring a notebook to make notes about what various exhibitors will tell you, as well as write down what breeders had cats you really admired. Additionally, you can see the cats in person to get an idea of what "look" and color of Persians you like best.

MAKING YOUR INQUIRY

Once you have done your research, it's time to start sending out inquiries to the breeders you have found meet your criteria. First, do not assume they have listed every cat they have available on their website. Many breeders do not update their own websites, so there tends to be a lag on their updates. Also, most top breeders will reserve their show kittens long before they have time to take pictures and/or place them on the website as available. So do not hesitate to inquire from a breeder that doesn't have cats/kittens listed as available.

In your first email to the breeder (and most breeders prefer email to phone calls), be sure to include an introduction about yourself. This doesn't need to be curriculum vitae, but you should include information about your general location, your past experience with cats (especially if you have any with the breed you want to buy for breeding), your intentions with your breeding program, and also what you are looking for from them. So many times, breeders receive inquires that read like this: "How much are your cats?" Most of the time, breeders will simply delete those emails. You don't want to be overly wordy, but remember you are asking this breed to entrust you with a quality cat from their program, a cat they raised from birth and planned for so carefully. So they are going to want to get to know you before they will sell to you (or they should want to get to know you. A red flag should be if a breeder isn't interested in getting to know you, just how much money you will pay them for their cat.)

Do not be surprised if they ask you to show a cat in the premiership class first. In fact, it's better to send out inquires about getting a cat to show in premiership class before you even start trying to find a cat for breeding. What is premiership class? It is a class especially for neuters and spays 8 months and older (registered, pedigreed cats).

Many new breeders start in premiership class, and there are many good reasons why it is the best way to start. First, it's an easy way to get a foot into the cat fancy without having to deal with the issues that come up with breeding. By showing (and titling) a cat in premiership, you demonstrate you are serious about exhibiting cats and this makes top breeders more willing to trust you with really nice cats. Second, the you can determine if raising and showing cats is really something you want to do before you actually commit a good deal of money into a program. Most breeders ask pet price for premiership quality kittens, though some will ask a good deal more (and those are the ones to avoid). Fourth, in showing a cat in premiership, a new breeder can observe many different looks of show Persians in the fancy and determine what look they

27

want to model in their breeding program. Additionally, you can talk to many exhibitors and pick up a wealth of knowledge at the shows that will aid you greatly in your endeavor of being a show breeder. Those breeders that might not have talked to you when you attended the show as a spectator are far more willing to open up to you as a fellow exhibitor. Finally, if the new breeder decides after showing a premiership that showing is really not for them, then they only have the one cat, which is already neutered and a great house pet, rather than having to deal with placing out many cats they might have bought/bred.

Once you have sent out your inquiries, the next step is: be patient. Some breeders get many inquiries a day and may not have time to respond immediately. In general, if you haven't gotten a response in about a week, most breeders wouldn't mind a second email (with the same information about the first, with a quick preface that you are re-sending in case the first email got buried in the inbox.) Never get terse with a breeder. That's a good way to end your chances with that breeder and any other breeders they work with before you've even begun. If you do not receive a response after the second email, it's likely the breeder is not going to respond and it's best to scratch them off your list and move on. If you really, really like their cats, you could try again in the future to see if you will get a response after you have gotten some more experience in showing & breeding.

PURCHASING YOUR FIRST CAT

Eventually, you will find a breeder and a cat you want to purchase. Before sending money, be sure to check that if they had a contract on their website, it is the same as the contract they will use with that cat you are purchasing. If you have any questions or concerns about the contract, now is the time to bring them up with the breeder, before money or cat has changed hands.

Ideally, you will be purchasing a premiership cat first, but if not, a male should be purchased before females. This is because males tend to take longer to breed than females, and it is a huge risk to the female to be cycling (in heat) and no male to breed her (or if your boy can't figure it out). In Persians, many males do not breed until they are 20-24 months of age. The females tend to start cycling around 10 months of age. The general rule of thumb is that you can skip the first two or three heats with the female, but if you skip more than that, she is at high risk of pyometra (a uterine infection that can lead to sterility and/or death.) The most ideal situation is to be able to purchase a "proven" male that a breeder has used for a few breedings and is now ready to part with. Of course, you will want to see the quality of his offspring, but oftentimes breeders are willing to part with a male that is 3-5 years of age, and a GC, for less than they would want for a comparable, younger male. That isn't to say you will be able to find one cheaply – a quality, GC titled male will probably still be $2000 or higher. But a proven male is invaluable to a beginner's program.

At the same time that you are preparing to purchase your first cat, you will need to be also searching for a vet. Your best source of information to find a good vet is local breeders. Find out who they use and who they don't recommend. There are vets out there who are not friendly to breeders (which does seem a bit ironic, since breeders are producing cats that will at some point, probably require their services and keep them in business.) There are also vets who seem to treat cats like they are small dogs; or they seem to believe that all cats can be treated the same way. Finding a good vet who is breeder friendly AND recognizes that different cat breeds need to be treated differently can be as difficult – if not more so – than finding a breeder to purchase a quality cat from.

You will also need to take the time at this point to invest in some basic cat supplies, including food (whatever the breeder is using is best), bowls, water bottles (if the cat is water bottle trained), litter pans, litter, basic meds, as well as preparing a portion of your home for your new cat (including caging)

Purchasing Additional Cats

After you have purchased and hopefully shown your first cat, it's time to consider adding cats to your program. Follow the same process as you have hopefully used for your first cat – research, research, research. Maintaining a good relationship with the breeder you purchased your first cat from is important, as they can be used as a reference with other breeders. Also, they can send you to breeders they know have nice cats and lines compatible with their own. You also now have a new avenue to research, and that is by talking with people at shows. Remember that new cats must be quarantined for a period of time to make sure they adjust to their new home and also to make sure they get a clean bill of health from your vet.

HOUSING YOUR CATS

Cats can't all simply run the house together – that is a recipe for disaster. Often times, I see in emails, websites, or posts, people bragging about their "cageless" catteries. And, rather than being impressed, I usually automatically think "Wow, irresponsible breeder." To be sure, none of us really want for our cats to live their lives in a cage. However, responsible breeders realize that there are times and/or circumstances where caging is not only necessary, but critical to the health of the cat. Cages come in all sizes and shapes. Here are things that I believe are important in a cage:

• "Clean-ability" – All surfaces should be sealed and scrub-able, preferably with no cracks or groves that food, litter, or other detritus can get stuck in.

• Floor space – Cats really need more room horizontally than vertically. The "tokyo" style cages really do not have enough floor space, they are usually 2 x 3 feet. Cages 5-6 feet in length or width (at a minimum) are much better.

• Wire spacing – Wires should be close enough that a baby kitten cannot fit through or get stuck.

• Shelves – Cats do like to jump, so there should be at least one shelf which can run the length of the cage.

The shelf should be made of a non-porous material and scrub-able.

There are other things to consider with cages, of course, but those are the main things to keep in mind.

Whole (intact) males

Whole males (or intact, un-neutered males) need to kept separate from other whole males and young kittens, as well as whole females that are not intended to be bred to them. Many times people will keep whole males together and insist there is "no problem." However, it only takes a moment when one of the males, or both, suddenly decides to become territorial/hormonal and attacks the other male. It can happen at any time and at any age.

A fight between two males is usually very violent, leading to death or severe injury, not just of the cat but of the owner too. Should you be unfortunate enough to have two of your males get in a fight, do not attempt to separate two fighting whole males with your hands, you will probably end up in the ER. Use towels or blankets to cover them and carefully separate - giving each cat time to "cool off" before you attempt to determine the damage that has been done.

Some people find it "very cute" to let whole males run with kittens. They often proclaim the males are "so gentle" with the kittens. Yes, they often are. But then sometimes, the males decide they have to breed that nine week old kitten - and they pounce on it. If the kitten isn't instantly killed, it is likely the spine will be broken in the process, and then you have a kitten you must put to sleep from an accident that a responsible breeder would have avoided. (This hasn't happened to me, but I have heard the horror stories from those it has happened to.) Additionally, in the case of a female that cycles young (5-6 months), a responsible breeder does not want that cat getting bred, so they cannot be kept around a whole male. If you don't want to know when kittens are due or who the sire of the litters are, by all means, allow the males to run the house all the time with your breeding girls. You'll end up with all kinds of surprises, including females getting re-bred just a few weeks after they birth a litter if they are one of those that cycles often. On the other hand, if you want to be a responsible breeder, males and breeding females should be kept/housed separately.

Whole males can be prone to bladder stones which can in turn block the urethra. The best way to catch this before it becomes serious or lethal is to know exactly how much urine a male is putting out each day. Males that run with other males - you never know how many of the pee spots in the pan are from each male. If they are with females, you won't know if any of the spots are even from a male. Males should urinate at least once a day, and not in small quantities. You can only monitor this if you separate your males. Since males really cannot run with other cats, the best situation for them is either a large "Walk-in" style cage with shelves and cat trees, or a room for them alone. If such things are not possible, then make time each day for the other cats in the house to be confined to allow the male to have "run time."

Pregnant & Nursing Females

Pregnant and nursing females need to be confined for both safety and health reasons. Usually pregnant females do not need to be confined until about the last 2 weeks of pregnancy, unless the female has a history of miscarriage. Pregnant females often do not consider their increased bulk and weight - which increase the most during the last 2 weeks - when jumping from one place to the next. As a result, sometimes they will try a jump and miss, which can result in severe injury and/or miscarriage. For the safety of the pregnant female, she should be confined in a cage - preferably without shelving - the last two weeks. This will allow you to monitor her closely as her time approaches.

I should note that often a "room" isn't sufficient confinement, especially for a female with a "high risk" pregnancy - one that has miscarried before, or one that is older (5 years plus), or one that appears to be carrying a large number of kittens and is huge. Humans with high risk pregnancies are put on bed rest, cats don't get that, so the next best thing is a smaller cage without shelving. Smaller doesn't mean that the female cannot move - at a minimum, she should still have 4-5 feet of horizontal space to walk.

Nursing females can often get "nervous" and start moving their babies around. Babies can get lost under furniture or mom-cats might move a few of the babies and leave the rest. It is best to keep the moms confined with the babies until weaning, at which point, the mom can start taking turns out of the cage. But be very cautious at this stage and never leave the mom outside the cage from the kittens or vice versa unsupervised. If the mom is in the cage and the kittens are out, the kittens will try to climb to her to nurse. If the kittens are in the cage and the mom is out, it is not unheard of for the mom to try to reach through the cage with her mouth, grab a kitten and try to pull it through the wiring. Queens and kittens can be severely injured or killed if separated by just the wire of a cage. You must carefully supervise and control the weaning stage.

There are many practical reasons for caging litters of kittens. Keeping the babies caged ensures they learn good litter box habits, as well as making for easier cleaning during this learning process. Cages with a hole in the floor for a sub-surface litter pan accelerate the kittens' learning by as much as a week. It's easier to fall into the pan than climb into it! If you need to medicate the kittens for sticky eye or a runny nose, you can more easily catch them in the cage. If they are in a room, they will quickly learn what you are trying to do and run, leading you on a chase that just makes them avoid you all the time as they become more and more frightened of you. If the kittens are confined, you have the upper-hand and can easily catch them when you need to, and they are less frightened when you handle them.

Additionally, litters of kittens should not be allowed to mix until they are much older, I would say minimum 12 weeks, but really, should be closer to six months! While it is really cute to see them run and play, kittens can pass around/swap germs as bad as a daycare. Even worse, their immune systems can get overstimulated/hyperactive, leading to FIP. For the safety and health of kittens, they should not be allowed to run together or with other adults until their immune systems are more mature. The exception to this is if you must take infant kittens from one queen to nurse on another. As I've already mentioned, kittens should never be allowed to roam with whole males, even when they are older. A male might "catch" an early-cycling female at 6 months and you'll end up with a kitten pregnant - something I'm sure nobody really wants. Worse, a male could harm any small kitten trying to breed it.

Show Cats

There are a number of reasons why caging show cats is advisable, including for the mental health of the cat. Yup, that's right, mental health. A cat that is allowed to run the house or a room is used to that freedom - and comfortable with it. If a cat is caged part of the time at home and allowed to roam part of the time, it will come to regard the caging time as either nap time, or worse, punishment. Should that cat then be taken to a show where it is in a cage, it will probably sleep or be generally unhappy the entire show. The owner will be unhappy. The cat will sense the owner's unhappiness and multiply it. It's a nasty little cycle.

Alternatively, if a cat that is to be shown is caged - all the time - that cat comes to regard the cage as "safe" and "normal." All things can be done in the cage - sleeping, playing, eating, etc. When that cat is taken to a show, it's in a cage - but that's not traumatizing to the cat. Rather - the cat feels "safe" in the cage and far more open to checking out the "new stuff" outside the cage. Mentally, the owner has prepared the cat for the show experience and lessened the stress and anxiety a cat might face at a show significantly. Almost always, when I talk to someone about their cat not liking the show, or sleeping during the show, their cat is one that is not caged or rarely caged at home.

When a show cat is no longer being shown, of course, caging all the time is no long necessary and certainly not expected. At most, show cats are only shown for 4-8 months, though some are campaigned longer. It's a relatively short portion of a show cat's life to remain caged - especially considering how much you lessen that cat's stress level by preparing it mentally for the show.

Another reason for caging show cats – grooming, especially Persians. Show Persians tend to be very groom- intensive. Running the house is a good way to break off coat, and lose that precious weight we want on our cats. Additionally, you will want to monitor carefully the food and water intake, as well as the stools, of a show cat, because they are more prone to illness due to traveling and exposure at shows. Exposure at shows is another reason why caging show cats is wise. At any given show, your cat is exposed to a number of fungal spores (there are different kinds), fleas, and airborne illnesses. Ideally, all cats at the show are in perfect health, but that's rarely the case! To be absolutely responsible to your home feline population, show cats should be isolated (their cages in another room) from the rest of the cats until their show career is completed and they have finished a quarantine time from their last show. Since many people keep their show room Persians in a cooler and darker environment than the rest of the cats (for promotion/retention of coats), it works out well as a quarantine room as well.

Ill cats

Anyone who is raising cats will at one time experience an animal (or more than one) becoming ill. These animals need to be separated from the other cats in order to limit exposure to the contagion as well as to monitor food/water intake and stool/urine output and catch easily to treat. You might be able to catch your cat easily normally, but cats intuitively know when you have a bottle of some medicine nearby and they run. If a serious illness should sweep through your home, you will need to cage every cat individually in order to successfully treat and hopefully cure each animal.

Naughty Cats

Again, almost every breeder will at one time have a cat that simply decides that litter boxes are "optional." For the sake of keeping your house clean and not having the floors ruined, these cats must be caged for "retraining." Sometimes, these cats never will use the litter boxes faithfully - and caging until such time that a very difficult decision must be made is about the only thing you can do with them. You can use diapers and stud-pants to allow such a cat outside of the cage when you are home to supervise.

In Summary

For those of you that say you are a "cageless" cattery but you do have cages and use them for any or all of the above reason - you are not a "cageless" cattery. While you do not cage your cats all the time, you cannot in all honesty call yourself "cageless" if you do in fact have cages and use them for certain circumstances. To advertise as such is to buy into the animal rights wacko's propaganda that confining a cat is bad.

I don't think we need to try to appease the animal rights wackos. Neither do we need to post on our websites "YES WE DO CAGE!" If a buyer inquires about caging in your cattery, you can honestly answer "My cats do not live in cages, but there are times when, as a responsible breeder, I do have to cage them for their health and that of the other cats in my home." And you can explain to that person what those times are. I believe we can help educate the public about cages and stop feeding animal rights propaganda machines with the "cageless" claim

SHOWING YOUR CAT

Most of the best breeders in the world believe that if you want to breed, you should show, because this is validation you are breeding cats to the standard. Many new breeders are just not interested in showing, but keep in mind that showing breeders are more than likely going to be just uninterested in selling to you unless you will commit to the exhibition of your cats.

When you purchase your first cat, it is ideal to do so from a breeder who lives near to you so they can help with the grooming, as well as be present at the shows to help with last minute grooming and explaining the show process. If that is not possible for you, the next best thing is to start asking local breeders if they are willing to help you get started in showing. Some will not have the time or inclination, but you are likely to come across some that are willing to step up to help mentor you. CFA does have a "Mentor Program" that you can apply to be assigned a mentor by CFA, but not all breeders who are willing to help are part of the mentor program (for whatever reason) and sometimes the mentor program can take months to pair you up with a mentor. If you have chosen to work with a "minority" breed, you will probably have a hard time finding a local mentor, at which point you will want to start looking on the internet and writing to people who work that breed, regardless of how far away they live. The internet is a glorious tool – be sure to use it to the fullest extent!

Hopefully, you have attended a few cat shows as a spectator before actually buying a cat, so the process of the cat show will not be completely foreign to you. There are certain supplies you will need prior to the show – such as cage curtains (if you are going to use to the show provided cage) or a show shelter (such as SturdiProducts). You will also need grooming combs, brushes, and powders, plus food, bowls, and water from your home. You will need a sturdy carrier to transport your cat, and probably a cart to move all your stuff in and out of the show hall in. (Shaving kit bags work great to hold the grooming "stuff.") Don't forget a litter box and litter for your cat to have in their benching cage. Here is a full list of what we bring to shows with us:

1) Grooming cart (carpet, on wheels). This serves 2 purposes - one, I can haul in carriers, plus stuff on top of the cart, and two, I have a place to groom in the show halls (spares the expense of a grooming space). It

has 4 bungee cords that I use to hold the top and bottom together.

2) Cage Curtains/Pop - UP cage. If I'm showing a rowdy shorthair, I'll bring out of the Sturdi cages because the shorthairs just tear up the curtains. Otherwise, I just bring curtains. I have a small suitcase I have all the cage curtains and accessories in.

3) Litterpans - usually these are in the carriers with the cats (I use LARGE carries), but sometimes I need a few extra. I will usually have a bag of litter I keep in the car in case I don't like the show hall litter.

4) Grooming Bag - this is a LARGE duffle bag with 2 large side pockets and 2 smaller pockets as well as the large main storage. In it I have a smaller "shaving kit bag" that I keep most of the main grooming, plus all

sorts of smaller bags for sorting. I'll list all the items outside of the kit first.

• no-rinse shampoo

• dry shampoo powder

• lint roller

• small wisk dust pan

• small medicine bag for cats containing basic antibiotics as well as anti-nausea and anti-diarrhea meds.

• roll of paper towels

• water bottles

• bottled water

• small bungees to attach water bottles to cages

• small and large binder clips for cage curtains

• "Please Do Not Touch", "Kittens For Sale", and "Cacao Cattery" cage signs

- Large metal toothed brush (it doesn't fit in the kit bag)
- roll of small trash bags
- toys, on sticks, balls, catnip.. ect..
- a cleaner for the litter pans (liquid)
- ozium (it's an odor neutralizing spray in case one of my cats makes a very big stink)
- small cotton pads for eyes (make up pads)
- cat food
- a couple of small bowls
- Summer's Eve powder (it's really good for a stinky male)
- Summer's eve spray (same ... good for stinky male)
- back up hand sanitizer
- human first aid kit

• assorted human dining ware (spoons, knives (not sharp ones, butter type knives) and forks.) You really never know when you might need one of these.

The "kit" bag:

• small "flea" comb (for under the eyes, chin)

• med 6 inch comb #1 (fine/med teeth)

• med 6 inch comb #2 (med/course teeth)

• 10 inch comb fine/course teeth)

• "slicker brush"

• various spray bottles with water, water with a bit of downy, bay rum, a spare for water...

• allergy eye drops

• moisturizing eye drops

• trip-antibiotic eye drops

• pill-pusher

- various powders - a couple of different "white" grooming powder, baby powder, corn starch, boric acid powder, and mennen talc (it's slightly pink for dilute cats)
- various make up brushes for applying aforementioned powders
- nail clippers
- round-ended scissors
- q tips
- business cards - mine and others
- some combination locks for the security cage if I ever feel uncomfortable with the gate in a show hall
- several pens, of which at least hopefully ONE works
- hand sanitizer (probably a couple of these, I lose them a lot)

- rescue remedy or some similar sort of "calming" homeopathic

If I am staying overnight, I will also take with me overnight cages and an overnight bag. The overnight cages are large (48x30) fold down soft-sided crates. I have a board that I bring that fits between them so I can stack them 2 high. The overnight bag contains:

• A small metro dryer

• A small pistol style travel dryer

• Shampoos/conditioners enough for clean up or touch up bath

• Hose/sprayer attachment

• Rubber wrenches for attaching the hose

• More bowls for food and/or water

• Incontinence pads to be put on the bottom of the crates

• Dry "kibble" food (I change this out every show).

To be honest, our show "kit" is more thorough that most. A basic show kit probably doesn't need even a fourth of what we bring. We tend to over prepare because you never know what you are going to need at a show. When I fly to a show, I take substantially less and hope if I need anything else, I can find it either at a vendor at the show or I'm able to get to a store. Key items I bring when I fly:

• Show curtains

• Metal combs (2 sizes)

• Pin brush

• Water "mist" spray bottle

• Litter & litter pan

• Food bowl & food

• Water bottle w/ stand or water bowl

• Pop up overnight cage

• Small metro dry & small amounts of shampoo/conditioner in case I need to do an "emergency" bath.

• Incontinence pads to be put on the bottom of the crates

Once you are ready for the show, the next thing is to actually enter & attend a show. Most, if not all shows, can now be entered with online entry forms. This consists of going to a specific link and filling out data on a web form. To fill out the entry form, you will need your cats green slip for information including registration number, date of birth, parents, and breeder. (If you have a kitten that is not yet registered, you can enter it in a show with no registration number, but any awards won without a registration number do not "count.") You will have to fill out some information about yourself, including your home address and contact information. If you have any problems filling out the form, or questions, you can contact the entry clerk (who will have their contact information on the online show flyer), your mentor, and/or your breeder.

Depending on what part of the country you live in, you will probably also want to mark "double cage" if you are only showing one cat. With the exception of some west coast show, all shows in the US use benching cages that are 48 inches wide. These cages have two openings and a metal wire divider that can be used to divide the cage in half. Each entry is allowed ½ of the 48 inch cage. That is really not enough room, so everyone with a single entry generally pays to have the whole cage (called a "double cage".) Some people also get a "grooming space" which is a 48 inch section of table without the cage. If you have a grooming cart or small table, you can skip this expense. There are a few rare show halls that do not allow grooming carts due to very narrow aisles. Also, some shows limit the number of groom spaces due to small show size. These are both rare circumstances and generally well noted on the show flyer.

Hopefully, you will have a mentor who is attending the same show and you can put their name as your "benching request" on the entry form. A benching request is just that – a request – but most clubs will honor them as much as possible. To be benched next to someone means your cages were be next to or near each other. This has several advantages. First, you have company to talk to, as one of the best parts of showing your cat is visiting with your friends and talking with other "cat" people. Second, you have someone who can guide you through the whole process and perhaps do some last minute grooming right at hand. Also, it's nice to have someone who can watch your benching area (and you watch theirs) when you are in a ring. Some show halls have a large amount of spectators who come through and it's always nice to know someone is keeping an eye on your cat(s) and possessions. Any valuables you bring into the show hall, such as your purse, wallet, cell phone, or camera should be out of sight whenever you are not around (and probably even when you to be safe.) Cage curtains with a "drape" that covers under the cage provides a handy place to put items out of sight. You can also tuck them away inside a carrier for added security. Some people will place the items in the cage with the cage, though they are still in sight if you choose to do that.

When you arrive at the show hall, the first thing you do is go to "check in." This is usually a table set up near an entrance (though perhaps not the entrance you come in) that will have a lot of catalogs set up and generally one or two people sitting there. Often there is a line. If you haven't yet paid for your entries, you will do so at this time. If you are paying by check, it helps speed things along if you have pre-written the check with the correct amount (the entry clerk will have sent you a confirmation with your amount due once you enter the show.) After you check in, you will be given a show catalog. You will also either be directed to a "benching chart" which has the general set up of the show hall with names written in on the spaces where the benching cages are, or given a row number to go to where your space is. When you check in, they will ask if you have any changes. Generally these changes are if a cat you entered will not present at the show, or if a correction needs to be made to your entry or entries (such as title, color, gender, date of birth, or competition class.) If you have a change and you forget to tell the person at check in, you can still make the change later during the show.

The first thing to do at your benching area is to set up your cage or cage curtains. It is important to be mindful of the aisle space and the area around you as you set up so that you don't block the aisle or crowd your neighbors. If you arrive early to the show hall (at the beginning of "check in" time listed on the show flyer, it is always easier to set up as there are less people. Once you have set up your cage or cage curtains, place the litter pan and any other items in the cage for your cat, then put your cat in the benching cage. It's important to give your cat time to adjust to being in the benching cage before you do any grooming (unless, of course, they have messed themselves in the carrier – that will require immediately grooming attention.) I usually use this time to familiarize myself with competition (listed in the catalog) and also with the number(s) assigned to my entry(ies). Most exhibitors will write their cat's number on their hand or wrist so they can remember what number is associated with their cat for that show. That number is how your cat will be called to the ring.

It's a good idea to also take a look around the show hall and locate where the rings are. For some show halls, this doesn't take much time, but in some areas, the benching and rings are in different rooms, so it is a good idea to figure out where you have to go to get your cat to a ring. Bathrooms, vendors, raffle, master clerk, and concession stand are also good to find before the show starts.

At the beginning of the show, a member of the show committee with introduce the judges, then call out the absentees/transfers (with information given at check-in.) Most people will mark these in their catalog as they are called out. Each catalog will have a sheet for absentees and transfers, usually located in the back of the catalog. After these announcements, the clerks in each ring will begin calling up cats to their rings. A judging schedule, usually located on the back of the catalog, lists the order each ring will call up cats. This is often subject to change due to conflicts causes by some judges moving along at a faster or slower rate than others, so don't only go by that. Listen for the numbers as they progress until your cat's number is called. If you have a cat that requires grooming, you should probably start grooming when the group of numbers is called before your cat's number. While clerks often do give 2nd and 3rd calls for numbers to a ring, it's a better idea to be in the ring after the first call.

In the ring, you will see that there are wooden blocks on top of the cages with numbers. Find your cat's number and put your cat in that cage. Before you enter the ring, it's always a good idea to pause to make sure you will not be in the way of the judge as you are putting your cat in the ring. Enter the ring quietly and get your cat into the cage with as little of commotion as possible. Some exhibitors use this time to fuss and play with their cat, but that is behavior that is generally frowned upon. After shutting the door to the judging cage, quickly exit the ring. At this point, you have to wait for the judge to get to your cat. Usually there are seats available in front of the ring, or you can stand to the side or behind the seating if all the seats are taken. Exhibitors are not supposed to talk to the judge in the ring, though sometimes judges will instigate conversations for a variety of reasons. Any conversations while watching judging should be kept quiet enough to not interfere with the judging process.

When the judge gets to your cat, they might use a teaser toy for to get your cat's attention and to get their first impression of your cat's over all expression, condition, and presentation. They will then take your cat out of the judging cage and carry it to the judging table. Many judges use this brief time between the cage and table to access the weight and body of the cat. While on the table, the judge will access type, color, and other aspects of the standard against your cat. Some judges do this very quickly; others will spend more time. This can vary from show to show depending on the number of entries and the format of the show. If your cat is frightened or timid, many judges will take extra time with your cat to make sure it has a positive experience. If you notice some aspect of the judging process seems to upset your cat, it's a good idea to repeat that part of the process at home so you can get your cat used to it before the next show.

After the judge has finished judging your cat, they will place it back in the judging cage. If your cat has competition, they will judge the competition, then hang ribbons according to how they believe the cats rank. Unless your cat is in a very large competitive class, it is like to be awarded at least some ribbons. Not all ribbons have points associated with them. The most coveted ribbon in class judging is the brown ribbon, which is best of breed or division. There is also an orange ribbon, which is 2nd best of breed or division. These ribbons will both convey points if won against competition. The last ribbon that can convey points is the purple ribbon, which is awarded to the best champion (or premier in the neuter/spay class.) The blue, red, yellow, black, and white ribbons do not convey points; they are for ranking purposes only. A red & white ribbon is used only in the Household Pet (HHP) class - it is called a "Merit" ribbon and confers no points.

When the clerk has dismissed your cat's class (either by putting the cats number down on the wooden block or by verbally dismissing the class), you can retrieve your cat and take it back to benching. Any ribbons on the cat's cage that are silk you can take with you if you wish. Ribbons that are laminated or plastic are permanent ribbons and not to be removed from the ring. If there are permanent ribbons on your cat's cage and you want the ribbons, there are usually silk versions of the ribbons on the clerks table for you to take. Sometimes a judge might want to speak to the owners when they remove their cats from the ring; remember whatever information a judge might want to impart is almost always meant to help the exhibitor. Also remember that a judge is completely in charge of their ring and it is against show rules to question the choices of the judge in their ring. If you feel a judge has acted or said something inappropriate, you cannot address that in the ring. Instead, you must first contact the show manager and follow the show rules from that point.

After a judge has finished judging all the cats in a category (such as kittens), they will conduct a final. In the final, the clerk will announce that the ring is having a final, and they will call certain numbers to come up to the final. If your number is called, proceed to the ring the same way you went for judging. After the final, the process is a little different. Rather than taking your cat and exiting the ring quietly, you pick up your cat, rosette/ribbon/award, and you thank the judge for the award.

This process is repeated for all the rings in the show. At the end of the day (or weekend), people will begin packing up and leaving, It's extremely important to do this quietly if rings are still judging cats. Also, make sure you do not leave before advertised show hours, as this is against the rules (unless you are only showing a kitten.) It's very important to make sure all rings you have competed in have actually done their finals before you leave. There have been many, many times that exhibitors leave early because they assume their cat will not make a final (or because they forgot they had a final to wait for) and the judge calls for their cat and they are gone. It's never a fun fact to find out your cat missed a final because you left the show too early. If you are not sure, it's better to wait to be sure before you leave. Sometimes, if you wait, your cat might make it into a final because someone else has left early and the judge will choose a new cat to complete their final – and that new cat might be yours!

If your cat does make finals at the show, your mentor or other exhibitors can help you calculate the points you have won by that award. The points are determined by a percentage of the cats competing at that show. If you aren't sure, CFA scores the shows each week and you can check the points with CFA. There is a subscription service for what is called "regional/national points" – these are points used the rank all cats for end of season award – and also a free service to track "grand" points (known as "Herman") which can be accessed at hol.cfa.org. Above all, remember when showing your cat that you are showing because you love cats. Sometimes, competition can cloud our judgment and we tend to get frustrated or upset depending on the wins or losses in the ring. Every show is different. Every ring can be different. Judges do not always have the same opinion. You might have different competition and the results may not always be the same from one show to the next. As long as you remember that you are there to have fun, to learn, and to socialize with your friends, you will find shows rewarding even if your cat isn't making all the finals or lots of points. Make new friends, help new exhibitors, and educate spectators about the beauty of pedigreed cat competition rather than just focusing on winning or beating the competition. By doing this, you will find you are less likely to get burned out by shows and more likely to enjoy the whole experience.

BREEDING YOUR CAT

At this stage, you have hopefully gotten some show experience, perhaps a title or two, and also have established at least one mentor/friend relationship with an established breeder. Now it's finally time to move on the next step – producing your first litter.

If your cats are just about any breed but Persian, this step generally isn't too much to worry about. Shorthairs, in general, figure things out quickly – and young. Our American Shorthair males sometimes can breed as young as 6 months (not that we want them to!) But Persians, as mentioned earlier, sometimes take a while to figure it out.

Hopefully, you have been able to acquire a proven male. That will go a long way in making this step easier. If not, however, you must learn to have patience. A young Persian male often is eager to try, but the first time the female "slaps" him, he will often back off and hide in a corner (often facing the corner.) A proven male knows better than to immediately "jump" a Persian female and generally will wait and "sweet talk" her. As long as the soon-to-be couple doesn't immediately begin fighting, this is where you have to give them some privacy. We've found that most pairings don't occur with virgin males while you are watching. The boy will be looking at you, wanting attention, rather than at the girl, especially if she has not be receptive to him. If you leave them alone, checking in every few hours if you must, you are far more likely to have successful breeding.

Additionally, unproven males that live with females are often less likely to breed those girls than males that have been separated from them, only to share time with them when the female is in heat. The boys that are too comfortable being "friends" with the girls seem to lack an understanding of what to do with them when the girls are in heat. Also, you don't really want your boys running with your girls all the time because this can lead to breedings happening when you aren't even aware (as covered in the "Housing Your Cats" section.

Assuming all goes well, mark your calendar on the first day you put a girl to live with a boy (note: always bring the girl to the boy, not vice versa.) Leave them together for 3 days or so, then remove the girl. At 21 days from the breeding date, you can check the girls nipples for what we call "pink up." That is, you look to see if her nipples have gotten larger and very very bright pink. You will need to have a look at the nipples before 21

80

days so you can tell if they have changed. This isn't as useful on older females as it is on first-timers (older, proven girls tend to have larger, pinker nipples even when not pregnant). A more reliable method is palpation, but it requires a good deal of teaching and a careful, sensitive hand. If you have a breeder who can teach you this method, do you best to learn it! Palpation can generally be used to detect pregnancy at 2 weeks, 3 days up to about 4 weeks. Before 2 weeks, 3 days, the kittens are too small to palpate. Past 4 weeks, the mother will be too fat to be able to feel anything.

Some breeders will take their cats to the vet for ultrasound to determine pregnancy. I don't really recommend that for a number of reasons. First, it's an unnecessary expense. Breeding is expensive as it is; if you can't palpate and can't tell by the nipples, assume the female is pregnant and plan accordingly. If she comes in heat again before the due date, then you can know she didn't take. Second, it's unnecessary stress to the female, and, by proxy, to her kittens if she is pregnant. A vet's office is often visited by sick animals, and despite the vet's best efforts, some types of infection still linger in the air and on surfaces. Why risk your female and your home cats? Finally, the ultrasound can leave you with the wrong count of kittens. A friend of ours some years ago was an ultrasound tech. She ultra sounded every single one of her cats and found that the count was never right. For some reason, some kittens are reabsorbed - in nearly every pregnancy. She'd count 4 kittens on the ultrasound, then panic when the mother only had 3 and rush her to the vet, only to find there were no more kittens. It's another unnecessary expense and stress to the momcat.

BIRTHING YOUR FIRST LITTER

Assuming all goes well and your female "takes", she will need special care, especially toward the end of her pregnancy. At about 7 weeks, a heavily pregnant female will need to be confined for her own safety (and that of her kittens.). If it is possible for you, see if you can attend a birthing with your mentor breeder (or any breeder who would be willing to allow you to view/attend a birthing.) This can prove invaluable when it's your turn. Also have a number of your mentor breeder to call should have you any problems during the birthing process when it's your turn.

At 63-70 days, your female should go into labor. She may or may not give you warning signs. She probably will give you many sleepless nights. Hopefully she will have her babies at a time you are home to assist, as first time moms, especially Persians, tend to not break the sacs on their kittens and leave them to drown. For the birthing process, you will need:

1. Lots of paper towels. I do mean LOTS.

2. A hemostat (clamp)

3. Clean towels (lots) for bedding changes

4. Rubbing alcohol

5. Scissors (sharp)

6. Bulb syringe

7. Cal-pho-sol or similar product/syringe to administer

8. A strong stomach if you are not good with blood

9. Mentally prepare yourself that it's possible you will lose kittens during this process, or that you might have one or more kittens born with birth defects

On the onset of labor (true labor – with contractions that make the whole cat move, or cry out, not twitching you think might or might not be contractions), note the time. It's important. If a female is in heavy labor for 2 hours and has no progression (no kitten, or a bubble that doesn't change), you are going to need to get a c-section.

Hopefully, progression will go smoothly. The first bubble you see generally is the "water". It will break and then you will either see nothing for a while, or a baby sac – which appears as another bubble – will be right behind it. NEVER try to break a bubble. The mother might do it herself, but don't do so yourself. Patience is important. Don't lift her tail and check every 30 seconds. Give her time. Be patient.

Correct presentation should be head first. Usually the mother can get the baby out quickly once the head is out. Be patient (I'll keep repeating this.) Don't pull on the baby! When the baby is completely out, you can use some paper towels to wipe away the fluid (and break the sac if it didn't as the baby came out) from the face of the baby. Don't attempt to take the baby away, as the placenta will probably still be in the mom. Once you are sure the baby is breathing and the excess fluid is wiped off, let the mother lick the baby and give her some time. It's very important to NOT PULL on the cord. The placenta will come out when it's ready. If you pull and rip the cord, there is a good chance the placenta could be "retained" and cause a severe infection for the mother. Sometimes the cord rips on it's own – make sure you count placentas later to ensure you have the same number of placentas as you have kittens.

Once the placenta is out (usually a few minutes after birth), you can choose to let the mom try to eat it, or you can remove the kitten at this time and take care of it yourself. If the mother eats it, it is good for her to get that nutrition, but I sometimes worry about the mother hurting the baby or chewing the cord off too close. Before you remove it, take a good look at the belly to make sure the skin is sealed around the placenta. There is always a chance the kitten didn't form correctly and what you assume is cord is actually intestine. This doesn't happen often, but it can happen. The cord should be whitish in color with a clear vein/artery running through it. Intestine is thicker and pink.

To remove the placenta, you should clamp the cord with the hemostat (or pinch with your fingers if you don't have one) about an inch or so from the belly of the kitten for about 30 seconds to 1 minute. Then cut the cord (with scissors you have cleaned with the rubbing alcohol and allowed to dry) on the placenta side of the clamp. Leave the clamp on for another minute or two and dispose of the placenta (or you can offer it back to the mother... chances are she won't want it.) At this time, you can sex the kitten, dry it off a bit more, and look for defects. In addition to the afore-mentioned problem with intestines/belly, look for a cleft palate. Gently open the mouth (I sometimes use a q-tip for this so I can swab out excess fluid that might be in there).

The roof of the mouth should be solid. This can be hard to tell sometimes if you have never looked in a kitten's mouth. Check all the kittens and compare. If a kitten has a cleft palate, it will not live long term. You have a hard decision to make. You can take the kitten to your vet to be put to sleep before it suffers, or you can let it linger for 3 or more days before eventually it will die (usually from aspiration pneumonia).

Should a kitten present breech (butt first), you might have to assist in the birthing. But carefully. It is helpful to have a 2nd person. If the kitten ends up about ½ to ¾ of the way out and the mother isn't getting farther, you will have to pull the kitten the rest of the way. The mother isn't going to like it, because she's already in a lot of pain and you will (temporarily) make it worse. She's likely to try to bite you; this is where the 2nd person comes in (to hold the mother to keep her from biting you.) Never wrap your hand around the kitten to pull! Instead, you must grasp the skin along the spine line (which isn't going to be easy – it's going to be slippery with birthing fluids and blood) and pull down and out. She'll fight you. You'll feel like you are hurting the kitten. But it must come out – and time is of the essence. Apply a firm, gentle pressure – don't jerk the kitten. When the kitten comes out, there is a good chance the cord will rip, but equally likely the kitten will not be breathing. Immediately wipe off the face and swab out the mouth. Use the bulb syringe to suck out as much fluid as possible from the nose and mouth. Rub the kitten briskly (but don't press hard) along the spine line to help revive it. As the kitten begins to breathe, chances are that more fluid will come out and will to be sucked out with the bulb syringe. There is also a chance that the kitten will not revive. If you cannot get the kitten to breathe in the first few minutes, then it probably will not revive. Even if you do get the kitten to revive, it might not stay alive for long. If it has aspirated fluid during the birth, it is at high risk for pneumonia and probably should be put on antibiotics immediately (amoxi drops or clavamox drops are both good choices.)

Labor for every cat can be different. Some mothers will have all their kittens in 1-2 hours, some will have one kitten, then take a break for 2-3 hours, then go back into labor to have another. This can be very frustrating! As long as the mom is out of active, heavy labor, try not to panic. If at all possible, refrain from moving a cat near or in labor. Moving them generally puts them out of labor and can significantly increase the likelihood of c-section and decrease the chances of survival for the kittens.

The cal-pho-sol (or equivalent) is vital for every breeder to have. It is used to treat eclampsia, or "milk fever." This is a potentially life-threatening disorder that can happen to nursing females. In simple terms, their bodies run out of calcium. But you can't just give them a shot of calcium; that could kill them. Instead, you use a balanced mixture provided in cal-pho-sol. Eclampsia symptoms vary, but generally the female isn't acting "right" – her balance might be off, rapid breathing, high fever. Since the shot is safe to give even if she isn't experiencing eclampsia, you can give a 3 cc shot if you suspect it. If her condition improves within 30 minutes after the shot, you know she is experiencing eclampsia.

Seek veterinary attention immediately once you have her stabilized. You can sometimes avoid eclampsia by making sure the mother has a lot of calcium-rich foods before birth and also in the weeks she nurses the babies. Goat's milk and cottage cheese both work well. There are also oral calcium supplements that you can give to cats (such as "oral-cal" gel.)

RAISING THE KITTENS

Getting your new mom and her kittens through the birthing process might seem like the biggest hurdle, but raising the kittens brings its own set of challenges and obstacles. Of course, sometimes absolutely nothing goes wrong and everything proceeds smoothly, but that isn't always the case.

The first challenge begins as soon as the kittens are born. It's always a worry until their mother calms down and lays with them without constantly shifting and potentially dislodging the kittens who are trying to nurse. The other part is – will the kittens nurse? We've had many anxious hours waiting for kittens to actually find a nipple and latch on. You'd think it was natural behavior, and for our shorthairs, it generally is, but for the Persians.. not so much. Some breeders will immediately offer their kittens a bottle (with newborn formula such as KMR), others will tube feed, and still others will refuse to supplemental feed at all. There are pros and cons to each. Bottle feeding before they nurse sometimes can lead to kittens totally dependent on the bottle. Tube feeding can easily be done incorrectly and that leads to a dead kitten (the tube can go down the trachea instead of the esophagus). Sometimes kittens just need a little extra help to get some weight on them and then they can nurse only. It's not something that can easily be explained or even written, but best learned by experience. This is again where a mentor breeder becomes an invaluable source to rely on.

As the kittens go through the first few weeks, it's important to change the bedding daily (sometimes twice daily) depending on how well the mother keeps them clean. Some moms will keep their babies spotless; others won't do a thing and it's up to you to potty the babies and sometimes wash their bottoms to remove fecal material. Also watch their eyes for signs of infection – new babies are very prone to eye infections, so watch for a yellow or brown crust around the eyes, or eyes that are "stuck" closed after the babies have opened their eyes naturally (which can take 5-10 days after birth.) Kittens with eye infections will need treatment – your vet can prescribe an antibiotic ointment.

When the kittens are about 4 weeks or age (or older, for Persians), they will begin to explore their surroundings, which includes getting out of the laying pan and not being able to get back in. It's important to keep a towel on the floor so the kittens have something to keep them off the cooler floor until you can get them back in the pan. It's important to keep the kittens and mother caged during this time as kittens can get "lost" under pieces of furniture – and a nervous mother might move her kittens multiple times, sometimes only taking a kitten and leaving the rest behind.

It's also time for them to start litterbox training. You will want a litterbox with shorter edges than what the mother usually uses so the kittens can get it in easily. If they can't get in, they'll start using a corner of the cage, and it becomes quite a chore to retrain them. Be patient for the first week or two of training – expect to need to vacuum the cage at least once a day and expect that the kittens will probably eat some of the litter (and play in it.) "Poop hockey" becomes a very good game for them.

Kittens will also start trying out the food and water that their mother eats. We've found if the mother has a wide, low food bowl, the babies will sometimes use that as a litterbox; so try a small foodbowl for the time while they are litterbox training (but one heavy enough they can't tip it over.) You can soak the dry kibble food in hot water for 15-30 minutes to make the food softer for the babies. Don't soak much – they won't usually eat a lot, and what they don't eat in the first hour or two should be discarded. If you feed raw foods, you can begin introducing them to that as well at this stage. Watch the size of the chunks of meat; too big and the kittens can easily choke to death.

Weaning generally begins around the age of 8 weeks but can take until 12-14 weeks, depending on the litter of kittens. Don't try to rush weaning, because if you try to early, it can severely distress the kittens and lead to them dying. It's more important to wean on their schedule than it is to wean on yours so you can sell them early.

Vaccination and worming protocols are outlined in many places; we strongly recommend following the AAHA protocols.

SELLING THE KITTENS

When your kittens are finally weaned, vaccinated, litterbox trained, and ready to go, it's time to find them new homes. You might choose to hold back one or two for your own breeding program, but usually most of the kittens you have born at your house are not suitable for your breeding program (you can't keep them all!) If you have people who were waiting for a kitten, contact them when the kittens are about 6 weeks old to ensure they still want a kitten. They will probably want pictures, so have those ready to send. Some will want to visit the kittens; this is up to you, but keep in mind that kittens at 6 weeks do not yet have fully developed immune systems or personalities. It's a risk to have visitors handling them. Should you not have homes all lined up for them, it's time to advertise. If you believe your kittens are show quality, it is best to have your mentor breeder evaluate them. Most breeders will not take you seriously if you try to advertise young kittens as "show quality" from your first breeding. They know that kittens that appear perfect as babies often fall part, type wise, as they get older. If you do have a kitten you think is show quality, it is best to plan on keeping that kitten until it is at least 4 months and take it to a show or two to see how it does. If the kitten does well at the shows, then you can make a valid claim of its quality.

You will also need to develop a sale contract. A sale contract is to protect both you and the buyer. Look at the sale contracts of other breeders and borrow from them (they all borrow from each other!) Don't outright copy a sale contract unless you get permission (it would be considered quite rude.) Remember to avoid the negative aspects of the contracts out there; don't put clauses in your contracts stating you won't sell to someone because they live in the same region, country, or continent as you do. Don't try to restrict what happens to the offspring of a cat you sell. When it's sold, it's sold. You have taken money for the cat and to expect to still be able to dictate what the new owner does with the offspring of that cat is completely unreasonable. Such clauses in contracts are ALWAYS broken at some point. And it leads to incredible angst and anger that can be completely avoided by not putting those clauses in the contracts in the first place. While we will always use a sale contract, we also remember that no piece of paper is going to make someone do "right" by our cat. If we think that we have to make a person sign a contract to do "right" with our cat, then we usually don't sell to that person. Use your gut; if you think a person is bad news, you have no obligation to sell to them.

If the kittens are not show quality, then you are going to want to find "pet homes" for them. Newspapers were once the only way to reach potential buyers; but the internet age has opened wide new avenues for breeders to advertise their kittens. Pursue and use the numerous online free classifieds that are out there; don't limit yourself to just one listing. Take lots of pictures or even better, video of the kittens to showcase your kittens. Also, you might want to invest the time (if you have the willingness to learn) to develop a website, or the money to have someone do one for you. I believe it's best to learn how to do a website for oneself – this allows you to make changes quickly, and saves a significant amount of money in the long run. Avoid the common pitfalls of putting too much bling on your website – keep it simple and elegant. People will generally not spend much time on a website that is "too busy." Certainly do not put sound files! In general, people rapidly will click away from websites with music. However you design your website in the end, keep in mind it is your first impression to most of the world to your cattery.

Remember at the beginning of the book about how I recommended you contact a breeder? Expect that 90% of your inquiries will be those "HOW MUCH ARE YOUR KITTENS?" emails. Potential buyers often are emailing multiple breeders and don't take the time to write about their home, their cat ownership experience, and any other pertinent information you might want to know before entrusting them with a kitten you have raised with love and care. Even if you make it clear on your website that you want to know this information, don't expect people to pay attention. It's up to you to decide if you will respond to those emails patiently and ask for the information you want.

Eventually, you will set up appointments for people to come and meet you and the kittens. If you live alone, it's best to make sure someone knows you have a visitor coming over. If you have a breeder friend who lives nearby, having them come at the same time would be best. Some breeders choose to meet potential buyers at shows in order to avoid the risks having strangers enter your home. Use precautions as necessary to keep yourself and your cats safe. Some of your potential buyers might live too far away to visit. These buyers might well be willing to pay for shipping, but keep in mind that is a risk to the cat/kitten – airlines are not going to love and care for your cat/kitten as much as you do. Be aware of temperature restrictions, and, if at all possible, find a service that can hand carry the kitten to their new home in the cabin rather than shipping cargo. New USDA rules might make you a "commercial" breeder if you ship even one pet kitten, so it's important to learn the rules before you begin shipping. It's always better to have the buyers meet you in person, even if you have to meet them at the airport.

Sometimes it isn't easy to sell kittens. The market truly is impossible to predict. You might have set your prices too high; you might just have bad luck. It's important to scope out the market before you settle on a price for your kittens. If you are stuck with older pet kittens, you will need to consider dropping your prices and reaching out to a farther market. You can also take kittens with you to the shows once they are 4 months in order to sell them.

CONCLUSION

If you have reached the point where you have raised your first litter or two successfully, maybe kept back a kitten or two, you are now moving into the "not quite a newbie" time as a breeder. The next few years will pass by faster than you think, and soon your original breeding cats are going to start getting to the age when you need to think about retiring them.

Ideally, it's best to retire a breeder cat at or before 5 years of age. It's much easier to find them new homes when they are 5 years or younger. They are probably certainly capable of breeding more years; but you have to consider your ability to care for them (and your other cats) should you keep them in your program past the age of 5.

As a courtesy, you should also offer your foundation cats back to the breeder before you neuter or spay them. Sometimes the breeder might want them back; usually they do not. It's important to make the offer, however, as courtesy is something you can never give enough to other people in the fancy. If you continually treat others with courtesy, it will come back you.

I don't mention keeping these foundation cats (or any other cats you retire from your breeding program) because it's far too tempting to keep them all. Often, we feel a obligation to give our cats a forever home ourselves. We have of course established emotional bonds with our cats, and letting them go is not easy to consider. However, consider this: If you keep them all, how many is too many? How many cats can you truly take care of properly? For each breeder, this number is different. When you first start breeding, 3 cats might be the extent of your ability. As you learn and become more experienced, you might find you can handle a few more, then a few more. But eventually, those few more become too many. Be honest with yourself and your limits. This is another time when your mentor breeder is important. Allow them to visit, and often. Things you might not have noticed as lacking or important an experienced breeder might see and be able to bring to your attention. A good rule to remember once you have reached a number you feel comfortable with is: in order to keep a kitten, you must place another cat. In order to purchase an outcross, you must choose a cat that will be sold. Maintaining a program within your limits is essential to the health and well-being of not just your cats, but also for you.

Made in United States
Troutdale, OR
10/24/2024

24093453R00066